A train is made up of a cab and then a line of coaches. The driver sits in the cab. Sometimes there is a cab at the back of the train, too.

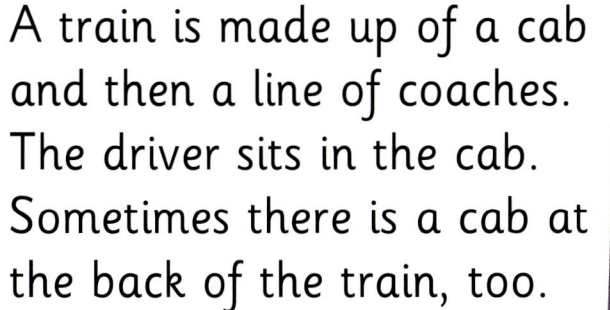

cab

train driver

coaches

The coaches are held together with a coupler.

All early trains had steam engines (/steem enjinz/). This sort of train was developed in 1801 by a British inventor called Richard Trevithick.

Trevithick lived in Cornwall. He used to take his friends for rides in a steam engine called the Puffing Devil, which went along the road instead of on a train track.

The Puffing Devil no longer exists. It was lost in a fire while Trevithick and his friends were having lunch.

Cornwall, in Britain

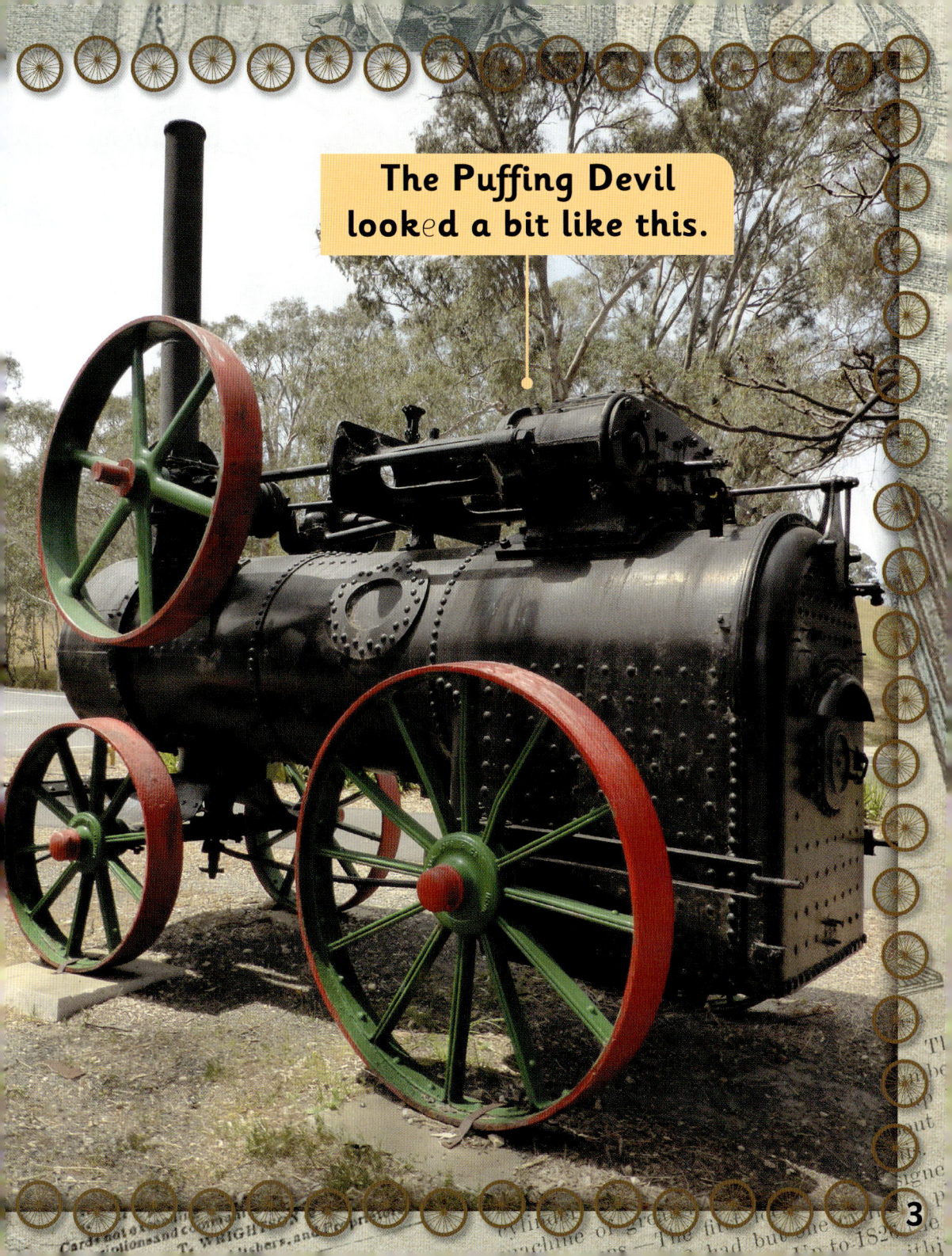

The Puffing Devil looked a bit like this.

Early trains were all fuelled with coal, whereas modern trains are electric or are fuelled with diesel. The electric trains sometimes have overhead lines.

lumps of coal

old train

modern trains

electric overhead lines

All modern trains run along a train track. The track looks like a long ladder that has been laid on the ground. There are metal rails and wooden planks, called sleepers.

sleepers

rails

The train's wheels run along the metal rails.

Look at these old and modern trains.

smoke box door

funnel

Old train

boiler

cab

buffers

connecting rods

wheels

Which parts are different and which parts are the same?

electric overhead lines

Modern train

cab

wheels

A lot of trains are used for public transport. They carry travellers where they need to go.

ticket gates

Everybody can ride on a train as long as they buy a ticket. Sometimes, you have to slot your ticket into the ticket gate to get on the train.

Then you can wait on the platform or in the waiting room before you catch your train.

If you see a pregnant or older person standing on the train, it is important to get up and let them sit down instead.

Some trains have beds in them. These are called sleeper trains, and they are normally used for very long trips.

There are bunk beds inside the cabins, so you can sleep as you travel.

bunk beds

Some trains carry cargo (things) instead of commuters and travellers. The trains in North America mainly carry cargo.

cargo trains

These North American trains carry oil, coal and mail across the country.

Some trains go very quickly indeed. The Shinkansen is a speedy Japanese train. It travels at an impressive 200 miles an hour, but the Maglev train goes quicker still. It travels at more than 370 miles an hour!

Shinkansen

These trains have long noses!

Funicular (/fu**ni**cueler/) trains are found on steep slopes, such as hills and mountainsides.

The steepest train track on the planet is for a funicular train in Switzerland.

In big cities (/**si**teez/), where there is not a lot of room, trains sometimes run in tunnels underground.

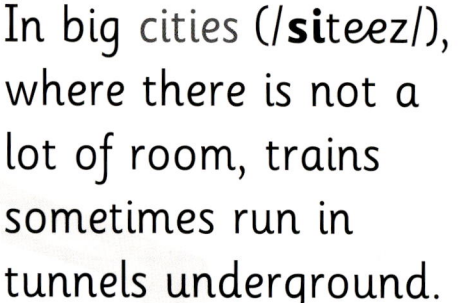

This is the tube. It runs under London (/Lundun/).

In Paris, the underground trains are called the Metropolitan, or Metro (/**Met**roa/).

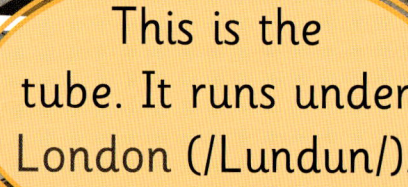

Sometimes, underground train tunnels can be very decorative indeed!

the Stockholm underground

In Stockholm, Sweden, the underground is decorated with art, paintings and rock carvings.

This underground tunnel in Russia (/**Ru**shə/) has golden tiles and columns.

If you like trains, there are lots of different jobs you can do.

1. The **conductor**, or guard, helps the train to go on time.

2. The **train driver** drives the train.

3. The **signalman** uses the signals next to the track to tell the train driver when it is safe to go, and when the train must stop.

4. The **ticket inspector** checks that everybody on the train has a ticket.